NEWS LITERACY

UNCOVERING
BIAS IN THE
NEWS

BY DUCHESS HARRIS, JD, PHD
WITH LAURA K. MURRAY

Core Library

Cover image: Two New York newspapers report the
news of President Donald Trump's election.

An Imprint of Abdo Publishing
abdopublishing.com

abdopublishing.com

Published by Abdo Publishing, a division of ABDO, PO Box 398166,
Minneapolis, Minnesota 55439. Copyright © 2018 by Abdo Consulting
Group, Inc. International copyrights reserved in all countries. No part of this
book may be reproduced in any form without written permission from the
publisher. Core Library™ is a trademark and logo of Abdo Publishing.

Printed in the United States of America, North Mankato, Minnesota
102017
012018

Cover Photo: Richard Drew/AP Images
Interior Photos: Richard Drew/AP Images, 1, 12; Steve Meddle/Rex Features/Shutterstock/AP
Images, 4–5; Leo Patrizi/iStockphoto, 6; Red Line Editorial, 9, 20; Shutterstock Images, 10, 24–25,
26; North Wind Picture Archives, 14–15; Joe Holloway/AP Images, 16–17; Andrey Burmakin/
Shutterstock Images, 18; Andy Dean Photography/Shutterstock Images, 28–29, 43; Andy Wong/AP
Images, 31; Nicolas McComber/iStockphoto, 34–35; iStockphoto, 37, 38–39

Editor: Patrick Donnelly
Imprint Designer: Maggie Villaume
Series Design Direction: Megan Anderson

Publisher's Cataloging-in-Publication Data

Names: Harris, Duchess, author. | Murray, Laura K., author.
Title: Uncovering bias in the news / by Duchess Harris and Laura K. Murray.
Description: Minneapolis, Minnesota : Abdo Publishing, 2018. | Series: News literacy | Includes
    online resources and index.
Identifiers: LCCN 2017947123 | ISBN 9781532113901 (lib.bdg.) | ISBN 9781532152788 (ebook)
Subjects: LCSH: Mass media--Objectivity--United States--Juvenile literature. | Press--Juvenile
    literature. | Journalistic ethics--Juvenile literature.
Classification: DDC 071.3--dc23
    LC record available at https://lccn.loc.gov/2017947123

CONTENTS

SIDES TO A STORY

The news anchor smiles into the camera. This evening's top story is the addition of hundreds of jobs to the area. The city council has just approved construction of a new sports stadium. The mayor says the stadium will bring visitors, jobs, and money.

In a newsroom across town, a reporter finishes her article. The story focuses on a group of concerned citizens. They are protesting the stadium. They say it will harm animals and the environment. The reporter includes other points of view. She quotes local

Different media outlets can cover a news story in very different ways.

Media organizations can reveal their bias through the stories they choose to cover and how they cover them.

business owners, an environmental expert, and a city council member.

Meanwhile, a blogger posts a photo online. The photo shows a destroyed beaver dam. His post says the stadium will harm local beaver populations. Within a few hours, the post has gone viral. The next morning, a radio host interviews the team coach, who is outraged. He cannot believe people oppose the project. He says the team needs the new stadium.

All these news outlets are reporting on the same event. But each account has a different bias. The varying approaches can affect how audiences understand the news.

MUZZLING THE MEDIA

Countries such as China, North Korea, Russia, Iran, Turkey, and Venezuela practice media censorship. These countries limit the powers of the press. They block or filter websites. They may shut down news outlets that criticize the government. They may even sue, jail, or harm journalists. Governments around the world also spread biased information called propaganda.

CONFIRMATION BIAS

A news story has various sides. But people often reject information or evidence that does not support their opinions. This is known as confirmation bias. David D'Alessio is a professor at the University of Connecticut. He says that people tend to notice bias that differs from their own point of view: "We know that, when people look at a story, they pick out the stuff that disagrees with them and . . . say, 'This is a biased story.'"

BIAS IN THE NEWS

News media outlets offer a massive amount of information every day. The Internet, TV, radio, newspapers, and magazines are all types of news media. Generally, people expect the news to be objective. Trustworthy news organizations aim to give complete and balanced accounts. They offer a range of viewpoints to ensure fairness and accuracy. They use multiple, diverse sources. And they try to be neutral so viewers can draw their own conclusions.

TONE OF NEWS
COVERAGE

Media outlets may try to remain unbiased. But their coverage shows otherwise. In 2012 the Pew Research Center studied how three cable networks covered the presidential candidates. Barack Obama was the Democratic candidate. Mitt Romney was the Republican candidate. How did the networks differ in tone? How does this help you understand news bias?

PERCENT OF STORIES WITH TONE

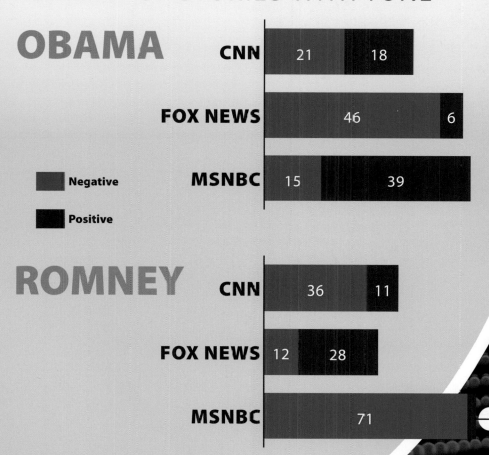

OBAMA

CNN 21 18

FOX NEWS 46 6

MSNBC 15 39

■ Negative
■ Positive

ROMNEY

CNN 36 11

FOX NEWS 12 28

MSNBC 71 —3

Daily News

Politics

Sed ut perspiciatis unde omnis iste natus error sit voluptatem accusantium doloremque laudantium

totam rem aperiam, eaque ipsa quae ab illo inventore veritatis et quasi architecto beatae vitae dicta sunt explicabo. Nemo enim ipsam voluptatem quia voluptas sit aspernatur aut odit aut fugit, sed quia consequuntur magni dolores eos qui ratione voluptatem sequi nesciunt. Neque porro quisquam est, qui dolorem ipsum quia dolor sit amet, consectetur, adipisci velit, sed quia non numquam eius modi tempora incidunt ut labore et dolore magnam aliquam quaerat voluptatem.

Nam lib nobis e impedi placeat omnis volu repellendu officiis debi et voluptat recusanda delectus, u consequati repellat. Se sit voluptat totam rem veritatis et

el eum iure,reprehenderit uptate velit esse quam e consequatur

Nemo enim quibusdam ipsam voluptatem quia voluptas sit aspernatur aut odit aut fugit

All media have some type of bias. Sometimes the bias is easy to spot. A media outlet may even advertise its slant. Other times the bias is subtle. It is up to the consumer to recognize it and to ask questions.

Bias occurs when news outlets allow opinion to affect the news and how they report it. They might favor one side. Perhaps they include interviews from just one perspective. The media also shows bias when it provides incomplete coverage of an event or issue. This can mislead its audience and lead to inaccurate conclusions.

MEDIA MATTERS

Not all news media are created the same. Some sources may consist of opinions disguised as news. Even trustworthy news sources contain different types of content. For instance, a newspaper contains news stories with straightforward reporting. It also contains advertisements and opinion articles. Readers must be able to tell the difference.

The 24-hour news cycle and explosion of media outlets make it hard to sort out the truth from biased sources.

News coverage is available in video form 24 hours a day.

Today people are getting their news from more places than ever. The news is available to the world 24 hours a day. Technology provides immediate access to stories, photos, and videos. This endless access to information also creates challenges. It can be difficult to sift through all the news and find the truth.

Uncovering bias in the news is an important part of being informed. The news media can influence our opinions. Responsible news consumers continue to ask questions. They dig deeper into what they see, read, and hear. They search for the full story.

STRAIGHT TO THE
SOURCE

Even the best journalists have some sort of bias. Author Alexandra Kitty writes that reporters have a responsibility to recognize their own biases:

> *News is supposed to present an accurate and truthful picture of reality. Watching a newscast is supposed to give the viewer the lowdown on what really transpired, who were the good guys and who were the bad. The trouble is that our wishes and beliefs continually cloud our assessment of what's really out there. The same biases that distort our vision also distort the vision of journalists. No one is truly safe from subjective biases, but an honest reporter takes extra effort to address his or her own personal prejudices before filing a story.*

> Source: Alexandra Kitty. *Outfoxed*. New York: Disinformation, 2005. Print. 65.

Consider Your Audience

Review this passage closely. Consider how you would adapt it for a different audience, such as your parents, your principal, or younger friends. Write a blog post conveying this same information for the new audience. Write the post so your audience can understand it. What is the most effective way to get your point across to this audience? How does your new approach differ from the original text, and why?

NEWS MEDIA EXPANDS

Media bias is not new. In the 1700s, American colonists wrote pamphlets and reports to help raise support for the American Revolution. In the 1800s, railroads and advanced printing presses arrived. These developments helped newspapers reach more people than ever. Many early newspapers were controlled by political groups. They promoted their own opinions and advertisements. In the 1900s, some newspapers began making a stronger effort to present objective information.

Bias has been a concern for as long as people have reported the news.

CNN's launch in 1980 marked the beginning of the 24-hour cable news cycle.

In the 1950s, television changed news coverage forever. For the first time, TV audiences could watch government leaders speak. They could witness current events unfolding around the world. The Vietnam War (1954–1975) became more controversial as the media shared more information about it. The public's support for the war became more divided. Media outlets began adding analysis to their reporting. Some people felt they could not trust the media to be objective.

24 HOURS A DAY

In 1980 the birth of Cable News Network (CNN) dramatically changed the media landscape. CNN was the first TV channel to show news 24 hours a day. People no longer had to wait for the evening news. They had continuous access to news. This was the start of the 24-hour news cycle, with headlines and reports being updated throughout the day as stories developed.

Opinion-based programming helps fill the schedule of many news outlets.

In 1996 another 24-hour news channel was launched. It was called Fox News. Fox News had a politically conservative view. It became one of the most popular cable channels. Another news channel, called MSNBC, began the same year. By the 2000s, MSNBC had decided to project a more liberal tone in its coverage.

The news channels started many trends that have spread throughout the media. They filled time with analysis and commentary. They featured live interviews.

They talked to panels for their opinions. They competed to be the first to cover a story.

MORE MEDIA

Today there are more media outlets than ever. There are more openly biased outlets too. Some organizations do not try to provide complete or objective news. They have their own agendas. Their news is misleading and inaccurate. Still, many of them have millions of followers, viewers, and subscribers.

IN THE REAL WORLD

OPINIONS IN NEWSPAPERS

Newspapers strive to be objective. However, most newspapers also have an opinion section. The newspaper's editorial board writes opinions on behalf of the newspaper. In 2012 *Los Angeles Times* editorial page editor Nicholas Goldberg explained: "For as long as anyone can remember, the editorial page has expressed the views and judgments of the newspaper. . . . We reach our positions through reporting, discussion, and, where possible, consensus. The publisher of the paper can get involved when he wants. The people who work for the news sections of the paper do not get involved in decisions about editorials."

CORPORATE MEDIA
CONTROL

Large corporations control most of the major media organizations in the United States. What do you notice about the number of companies that control the media? How might this play a role in media bias?

TIME WARNER

- CNN
- Cartoon Network
- DC Comics
- HBO
- TBS
- TNT

COMCAST

- Dreamworks Animation
- Universal Pictures
- Telemundo
- Weather Channel
- NBC
- USA Network

VIACOM

- Comedy Central
- Paramount Pictures
- Nickelodeon
- MTV

CBS CORPORATION

- CBS
- CBS Sports Network
- Showtime
- Simon & Schuster

21ST CENTURY FOX

- Fox News Channel
- Fox Sports Network
- National Geographic
- FX

WALT DISNEY COMPANY

- ABC Television Network
- Disney Channel
- ESPN
- Marvel
- Walt Disney Pictures
- Pixar

In the United States, a handful of corporations own most major media organizations. These big companies own ABC, CBS, CNN, Fox News, MSNBC, NBC, and more. This means that a few companies decide what news to cover. News networks also compete for ratings, advertisers, and profits. This can affect their biases. Sometimes people refer to the traditional news outlets as the mainstream media.

FORMS OF BIAS

Media bias takes many forms. A news outlet may leave out certain facts. It may rely on biased sources. One outlet may put

PLAYING FAIR

In 1949 the US Federal Communications Commission (FCC) instituted the Fairness Doctrine. It required TV and radio broadcasters to devote part of their airtime to coverage of controversial issues that were important to the public. It also required them to provide opposing viewpoints. Critics said the policy went against the First Amendment. The First Amendment ensures freedom of speech, among other rights. The FCC ended the Fairness Doctrine in 1987.

a news item on its front page. Another may bury the information in the back of the paper. Some channels may devote large amounts of time to a story. Other outlets may include only a brief mention of it.

The news can be biased in its politics. It can be biased in other ways, too. It may have a biased worldview. For example, news in the United States often reflects its own country's interests. People of other countries, backgrounds, or cultures may see events differently.

Words can show bias. One news outlet may label a suspect as a "troubled teen." Another might call him a "criminal." Still another news outlet could call the same boy a "local student." These terms might all be true. But they paint a very different image of the same person. They may influence opinions of his guilt.

STRAIGHT TO THE
SOURCE

Language can influence how an audience perceives a topic. Author Erika Falk discusses how media bias can affect public opinion about female political candidates:

[Studies] show the importance of what the media write about, how they write, and the language they use. . . . It is important because if the press always mentions what women wear, it may convey the impression that women are not serious candidates. It is important because if women are described by their emotions, it may falsely imply that women are not rational enough to lead. It is important because if women are always mentioned in relation to their families instead of their professions, they may appear less qualified for or dedicated to office.

Source: Erika Falk. *Women for President: Media Bias in Eight Campaigns.* Urbana, IL: University of Illinois Press, 2008. Print. 29.

Back It Up

The author of this passage is using evidence to support a point. Write a paragraph describing the point the author is making. Then write down two or three pieces of evidence she uses to make the point.

CHAPTER
THREE

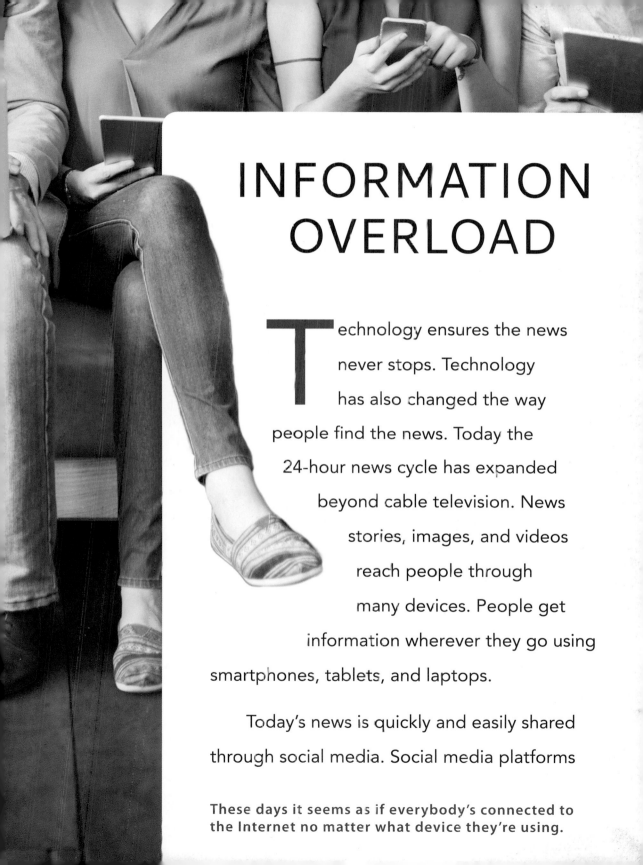

INFORMATION OVERLOAD

Technology ensures the news never stops. Technology has also changed the way people find the news. Today the 24-hour news cycle has expanded beyond cable television. News stories, images, and videos reach people through many devices. People get information wherever they go using smartphones, tablets, and laptops.

Today's news is quickly and easily shared through social media. Social media platforms

These days it seems as if everybody's connected to the Internet no matter what device they're using.

include Facebook, YouTube, Twitter, Instagram, Tumblr, and Snapchat. These platforms connect people around the globe. They provide instant access to information, sharing, and streaming.

However, social media and the Internet can add to an effect called the echo chamber. This is when people pay attention only to information that supports their

IN THE REAL WORLD

NEW CHALLENGES

People have more information available to them than ever. But they may not be better informed. James Klurfeld and Howard Schneider of Stony Brook University write: "The great irony of our time is that there is more information available at our fingertips than anytime in human history, but less and less confidence in that information. Rather than being better informed because of the [increase] of easily available information, studies show news consumers are less informed on key issues of public policy. And the problem has only become more acute with the explosion of social media and mobile technology."

It's important to be skeptical of news sources you suspect might be biased.

beliefs. A person's social media newsfeed is affected by his or her friends' shares. And users' own clicks shape what stories they see. Online algorithms also affect the stories that are displayed.

A DIGITAL WORLD

Traditional news outlets have changed to keep up with technology. They post stories to their websites. They are active on social media. They share eyewitness images and videos. They record videos of their own.

Technology gives people access to all sorts of information. But it does not guarantee quality information. In some cases, news may be inaccurate. In other cases, news may be recycled, out of date, or shallow. A news network could spend hours covering a popular issue. However, it may not offer any new information.

The information at the bottom of the screen is part of the message in a TV news report.

BIASED CAPTIONS

TV news networks often show chyrons, or captions, on the screen. Networks may insert bias in their chyrons. This happens even during live footage. An example occurred in June 2017. Former FBI director James Comey was testifying to the Senate. A chyron on CNN highlighted Comey's statement that President Donald Trump lied. Meanwhile, chyrons on Fox News were different. They put the president in a positive light.

Technology can add to the difficulty in identifying bias. It is easy to make ads or biased content look like news. Native advertising is paid or sponsored content. The ads look like the surrounding content from the media outlet. They might be articles or videos. Native ads often appear on the home pages of news sites. Sometimes the ads are marked as "sponsored" or "promoted."

PUTTING NEWS INTO CONTEXT

Technology allows anyone to create and share news. But the news can easily become distorted. Social media helps rumors, biased reports, and incomplete videos

A smartphone's video function can turn anyone into a "citizen journalist," but not all video should be viewed as credible.

go viral. People may take an inaccurate story as fact. They share it without considering the context. A story's popularity does not necessarily ensure its credibility.

A viral photo or video may show only a piece of the entire story.

Sources are an important part of context. Some news content is created by professional journalists. Other content is made by companies or biased groups. Hoaxers spread false information on purpose. Some news reports are meant to be satire. Humor websites and comedy news shows can be examples of satire.

Today's news includes content from citizens who are not professional journalists. News outlets often feature citizens' photos and videos. Other user content includes blog posts, podcasts, videos, and Internet forums. Even politicians create their own digital content. They send out tweets, make videos, and post memes.

SMALL BITES

News organizations want to keep viewers' attention. The news often features short recorded clips. These are called sound bites. Usually, sound bites do not contain much information. They are chosen for being catchy or memorable.

Sound bites are getting shorter and shorter. Today's technology allows speeches to be edited more easily than in the past. In 1968 the average televised sound bite of a presidential candidate on the evening news lasted 43 seconds. By 1988 it averaged nine seconds. Biased news reports take sound bites out of context. They use the sound bites in unfair or misleading ways.

EXPLORE ONLINE

Chapter Three discusses technology's role in media bias. The article at the website below has more information on this topic. How is the information from the website the same as the information in Chapter Three? What new information did you learn from the website?

SHRINKING SOUND BITES
abdocorelibrary.com/uncovering-bias

DIGGING DEEPER

I t can be challenging to uncover bias in the news. But there are ways to check on whether you are receiving a balanced account. When reading or watching a news story, keep asking questions. Understand what type of media you are consuming. A news report is different from an opinion or an advertisement. Keep in mind that advertisements can look like real news. If an article seems to be promoting a product, it could be an ad. Ask yourself who the audience is.

Check the source. If the news is posted to a website, visit the "About Us" page to

It's a good idea to compare how different sources report the same story.

learn about the organization. Glance at the site's other articles. They might reveal a certain slant.

Identify the author. What makes her an authority? Does she seem to be open-minded and balanced? Or does she have a connection to the topic? It could be a red flag if there is no contact information listed.

Pay attention to the sources within the story. Does the author cite his sources? Does he include more than one viewpoint? Is there a reason a source might be unnamed? Look at the evidence offered. Can it be proved? If the author cites a study, check the study out for yourself. A news channel may interview a panel of experts. What makes them experts?

GOING VIRAL

It can be tempting to share a viral image or story. But these are not always credible. Pictures and videos can be easily altered. Sometimes outdated stories resurface on the Internet. Verify the date and relevance. Then check into the source and content.

When a public figure is interviewed, think about why the reporters ask certain questions and why others aren't asked.

THE WHOLE STORY

It is important to consume news from different sources. Check out other sources to decide if a story is fair and accurate. Do the other sources support the information? Do they offer new views or details?

When news is breaking, sometimes media outlets get facts wrong in the rush to be first.

Note what information is missing. Might there be other sides to the story? Was the story unclear or hard to understand? Be skeptical of shocking headlines. Notice the words or images used. If they seem designed to make people angry or emotional, it is likely a biased story.

News outlets often share breaking news. Quality
news organizations tell viewers that the story is
developing. They highlight what is unknown. They
give updates and corrections. Unreliable outlets rush
to be first. That means they often share incomplete
news. This can mislead their audiences. The rush to

IN THE REAL WORLD

ASKING QUESTIONS

Questions are key in uncovering news bias. Tom Rosenstiel of the American Press Institute recommends asking these questions: What kind of content is this? Who and what are the sources cited? Why should I believe them? What's the evidence and how was it vetted? Is the main point of the piece proved by the evidence? What's missing? Rosenstiel writes: "When you decide what to click on, what to read, and when you lose interest and stop reading, you are making critical decisions about what matters and what you trust or what you don't understand."

cover a story can lead to the spread of inaccurate information.

SEARCHING FOR THE TRUTH

Different resources can help uncover bias. Librarians and teachers have tips and tools for finding balanced accounts. Fact-checking websites can also help. Think about your own news habits. Are you paying attention only to stories that support your beliefs?

Today some people mistrust the traditional media. Politicians and others may try to discredit news stories. However, there are still many journalists who strive to give fair and accurate accounts.

It is more challenging than ever to know what information is accurate. Responsible news consumers should be skeptical. The more you look for bias, the easier it is to identify. However, the truth is rarely so black-and-white. There are many sides to a story. It is up to each of us to ask questions and dig deeper to make up our own minds.

FURTHER EVIDENCE

Chapter Four has information on how to uncover news bias. What was one of the main points of this chapter? What key evidence supports this point? Read the article at the website below. Does information on the website support the main point of this chapter? Does it present new evidence?

QUESTIONS TO EVALUATE MEDIA
abdocorelibrary.com/uncovering-bias

FAST FACTS

- News bias can affect how audiences think about the news.

- All media outlets have some sort of bias.

- In 1980 the launch of the 24-hour news channel CNN changed TV news forever.

- Media bias takes many forms. It may promote or hide certain aspects of a story.

- Technology has changed the way people consume news.

- Social media platforms allow people to share news easily. This can allow for the spread of misleading or distorted information.

- People have access to more information than ever. That information is not always of high quality.

- People use technology to create their own content.

- Sound bites are short and do not contain much information.

- News consumers should be aware of confirmation bias and the echo chamber effect.

- It is important to verify news using several sources.

- Viral content can be inaccurate or misleading.

- News consumers should ask questions and continue to dig deeper.

NEWS

TRUMP ELECTED U.S

FL PRESIDENT

R TRU
D CL

AP
15
NTON

STOP AND
THINK

Tell the Tale

Chapter Four discusses how to uncover bias in the news. Imagine you are reading an article online. Write 200 words about the experience. What types of things do you need to keep in mind to uncover bias?

Surprise Me

Chapter Three discusses technology's role in media bias. After reading this book, what three facts about media bias and social media did you find most surprising? Write a few sentences about each fact. Why did you find each fact surprising?

Dig Deeper

After reading this book, what questions do you still have about the corporations that own media companies? With an adult's help, find a few reliable sources that can help you answer your questions. Then write a paragraph about what you learned.

GLOSSARY

agenda
the plan or motives of a group or person

algorithms
step-by-step methods; social media algorithms filter and select content for users

bias
favoring one side over another

context
the setting or circumstances that help clarify meaning

doctrine
a principle of government policy

irony
a situation in which reality is different than what is expected

memes
images, videos, phrases, or ideas that spread across the Internet

objective
neutral; unbiased

satire
the use of humor to ridicule or criticize

skeptical
doubtful of something's truth

subjective
based on opinion; biased

viral
quickly and widely spread

ONLINE
RESOURCES

To learn more about bias in the media, visit our free resource
websites below.

Visit **abdocorelibrary.com** for free Common Core resources for teachers
and students, including vetted activities, multimedia, and booklinks, for
deeper subject comprehension.

Visit **abdobooklinks.com** for free additional online weblinks for further
learning. These links are routinely monitored and updated to provide
the most current information available.

LEARN
MORE

Harris, Duchess. *The Fake News Phenomenon*. Minneapolis, MN: Abdo
Publishing, 2018.

Williams, Mary E., ed. *Media Bias*. Farmington Hills, MI: Greenhaven
Press, 2011.

ABOUT THE
AUTHORS

Duchess Harris, JD, PhD
Professor Harris is the chair of
the American Studies Department
at Macalester College. The author
and coauthor of four books (*Hidden
Human Computers: The Black Women
of NASA* and *Black Lives Matter* with
Sue Bradford Edwards, *Racially Writing
the Republic: Racists, Race Rebels, and
Transformations of American Identity* with
Bruce Baum, and *Black Feminist Politics
from Kennedy to Clinton/Obama*), she
has been an associate editor for *Litigation News*, the American Bar
Association Section's quarterly flagship publication, and was the first
editor-in-chief of *Law Raza Journal*, an interactive online race and the
law journal for William Mitchell College of Law.

She has earned a PhD in American Studies from the University of
Minnesota and a Juris Doctorate from William Mitchell College of Law.

Laura K. Murray
Laura K. Murray has written more than 40 nonfiction books
for children. She has also written for newspapers. She lives
in Minnesota.

INDEX